Tana Hoban

Is It Larger? Is It Smaller?

Greenwillow Books
New York

Library of Congress Cataloging in Publication Data
Hoban, Tana.   Is it larger? Is it smaller?
Summary: Photographs of animals and objects in larger
and smaller sizes suggest comparisons between the two.
1. Size perception—Juvenile literature.   [1. Size]   I. Title.
BF299.S5H63   1985   132.1'42   84-13719
ISBN 0-688-04027-6   ISBN 0-688-04028-4 (lib. bdg.)

THIS ONE IS

FOR MY FATHER

WHO TOLD ME

I WAS WONDERFUL